Fall 2015 Class

..‖ FORGOTTEN POWER ‖..
A Simple Theology for a Praying Church

David Butts

PRAYERSHOP
PUBLISHING

Terre Haute, IN

PrayerShop Publishing is the publishing arm of Harvest Prayer Ministries and the Church Prayer Leaders Network. Harvest Prayer Ministries exists to transform lives through teaching prayer. Its online prayer store, www.prayershop.org, has more than 400 prayer resources available for purchase.

ISBN: 978-1-935012-64-1

1 2 3 4 5 | 2019 2018 2017 2016 2015

··∥ TABLE OF CONTENTS ∥··

INTRODUCTION

..⫼ A THEOLOGY ⫼..

THE SUBTITLE OF THIS BOOK can seem a bit pretentious. "A Theology of a Praying Church." The use of the word "theology" for a little paperback like this doesn't seem to fit. We think of theologies as deep and long and something for scholars to study and argue over.

I began this work several years ago with a desire to develop a serious theology of prayer. An interesting thing happened as I studied and wrote though. My thinking and writing became shorter instead of longer, and simpler instead of more profound. I realized that the Spirit of God was doing a work in me, showing that most theology is intended for the simplest of people. We often try to take a clear message and confuse it by our scholarly language and our desire to convince by our words.

After spending several decades traveling to hundreds of churches, teaching on prayer, I have come to realize that virtually everyone is for prayer, but they don't know why. That comes from a lack of clear thinking about prayer. Clear thinking about prayer is what I call a theology of prayer. Those thoughts must be based on the Word of God, but still, we must take what the Word says regarding prayer, and carefully consider it if we are to become a people of prayer.

I know that some will counter that we just need to do it. Just **VIRTUALLY** pray. Of course, simply studying prayer without **EVERYONE IS** praying is worthless. But it is the combining of **FOR PRAYER,** clear thinking on prayer with the actual practice **BUT THEY** of prayer that is powerful. That's why the disciples **DON'T KNOW** came to Jesus and asked Him to teach them to **WHY.** pray. He didn't respond by saying they didn't need to be taught. He gave them a model prayer with very clear, practical principles that would help them form powerful, effective prayers.

.: PRAYING TOGETHER :.

As we learn to think deeply about biblical teaching on prayer, we discover that it's not just an individual matter, but a corporate issue. Especially in the United States, we have made our faith purely personal rather than corporate or for groups. The Bible certainly teaches about individual prayer, but it also has much to say about people praying together.

The "forgotten power" in the title, especially refers to the Church learning together what it means to pray. Much power has been ignored by the Church because of its failure in the area of corporate prayer.

W. A. McKay wrote of this power:

> When Elijah prayed, the nation was reformed; when Hezekiah prayed, the people were healed; when the disciples prayed, Pentecost appeared; when John Wesley and his companions prayed, England was revived; when John Knox prayed, Scotland was refreshed; when the Sabbath-school teachers at Tannybrake prayed, eleven thousand were added to the Church in one year; when Luther prayed, the papacy was shaken; when Baxter prayed Kidderminster was aroused; and in the lives of Whitefield, Payson, Edwards, Tennent, whole nights of prayer were succeeded by whole days of soul-winning. To your knees, then ye Christians! Plead until the windows open, plead until the springs unlock, plead until the clouds part, plead until the rains descend, plead until the floods of blessing come. (*Outpourings of the Spirit*, p. 136)

My prayer is that this little book, with its pretentious title, will be used by the Spirit of God to help us all see prayer from the Lord's perspective. As we gain that viewpoint, our task will be to surrender to the Lord's call to become a people of prayer that He can use to accomplish His purposes on this planet.

CHAPTER ONE

..‖ GOD'S NAME FOR US ‖..

The prayer meeting was to begin at 7:00 pm. So why were people lined up on the sidewalk at 5:00 pm waiting for the doors to the church to open? I couldn't believe my eyes. It was a cold December in Brooklyn, New York, and people were huddled together waiting to come into a prayer meeting. That had not been the case in my previous church prayer meeting experiences! But it was Tuesday night at Brooklyn Tabernacle and it was time to pray.

By 7:00 pm the building was filled to overflowing capacity. The next two hours were filled with amazing times of worship and prayer.

That night was not an exception, but the norm at Brooklyn Tab. Every Tuesday, the Brooklyn Tabernacle congregation models a wonderful way for a church to gather in prayer. The power of God is poured out as the people of God seek Him together in prayer. Jim Cymbala

THE CHOOSING of a name is very important. We all know parents who agonize over what to name their new baby. Communities often have many meetings and long discussions over how to name a new facility in their town. Biblically, the choosing of a name often gave special significance or meaning to a person or place. The name was so important, that when there was a change in circumstances, it often meant a name change was necessary.

In Genesis 28, Jacob had an amazing encounter with God in a dream. When he awakened, he renamed the place. "He called the place Bethel, though the city used to be called Luz" (Genesis 28:19). Both Jacob and his father Abraham had name changes given by God. In Genesis 17:5, Abram is changed to Abraham and in Genesis 35:10, Jacob becomes Israel.

Any name is important, regardless of who gives it. But there is special significance when God Himself steps in to name someone or something. That would be especially true when God names something that is particularly close to His heart.

∴ HOUSE OF PRAYER ∴

The Bible tell us that God has chosen a name for His own house. In Isaiah 56:7, the Lord says, "These will I bring to my holy mountain and give them joy in my *house of prayer.* Their burnt offerings and sacrifices will be accepted on my altar; for my house will be called a *house of prayer* for all nations" (emphasis added).

This straightforward naming of the house of God (House of Prayer) is simply a clarifying of what God had already declared concerning His house. In the amazing encounter that Solomon had with God at the dedication of the Temple, God made it clear that this was to be a place of prayer. Solomon prayed in 2 Chronicles 6:40, "Now, my God, may your eyes be open and your ears attentive to the prayers offered in this place." God's response in 2 Chronicles 7:15 is a resounding "YES" to that request.

Of great importance to us is the fact that Jesus took this naming seriously. Three of the gospel writers mentioned that Jesus quoted it and all four recorded the cleansing of the Temple where Jesus referred to His Father's words (Matthew 21:13; Mark 11:17; Luke 19:46; John 2:17). The fact that the Father's house was to be a house of prayer for all nations was so central to God's plan on earth that Jesus responded to Israel's failure in regard to this with a rare display of godly anger. Evidently, Jesus believed that the people who were a part of God's house should live in accordance with the naming of the house.

This becomes especially relevant to us when we understand that God's house was not in any way limited to the Temple in Jerusalem. God's house existed long before the Temple or its predecessor, the Tabernacle of Moses. And it exists even now and will continue when this age is over and earth ceases to exist in its current form. It is an eternal house and is

JESUS BELIEVED THAT THE PEOPLE WHO WERE A PART OF GOD'S HOUSE SHOULD LIVE IN ACCORDANCE WITH THE NAMING OF THE HOUSE. forever a place of communion with God.

The Bible is filled with references to God's house. As you read through these verses it becomes very clear that His house has never been limited to a building. The building was an important visual illustration of what it means to draw near to God and to dwell in His presence. Even at the dedication of the first Temple, Solomon realized this fact as he prayed, "But will God really dwell on earth with humans? The heavens, even the highest heavens, cannot contain you. How much less this temple I have built!" (2 Chronicles 6:18).

As we begin to understand that the Church today, both corporately and individually, is God's house, it is critical that we comprehend what it means to live in or be a house that has been named by God as a house of prayer.

Paul made it clear that we are God's house in Ephesians 2:21-22: "In [Jesus] the whole building is joined together and rises to become a holy temple in the Lord. And in him you too are being built together to become a dwelling in which God lives by his Spirit."

Paul really emphasized this fact to the Corinthian church:

"Don't you know that you yourselves are God's temple and that God's Spirit dwells in your midst?" (1 Corinthians 3:16)

"Do you not know that your bodies are temples of the Holy Spirit, who is in you, whom you have received from God?" (1 Corinthians 6:19)

"For we are the temple of the living God. As God has said: 'I will live with them and walk among them, and I will be their God, and they will be my people.'" (2 Corinthians 6:16)

Peter continues this teaching in 1 Peter 2:5, "you also, like living stones, are being built into a spiritual house to be a holy priesthood." The

Apostle John records the words of Jesus in Revelation 3:12: "The one who is victorious I will make a pillar in the temple of my God." In the Gospel of John we hear Jesus say to us: "Anyone who loves me will obey my teaching. My Father will love them, and we will come to them and make our home with them" (John 14:23). Can there be any doubt that the Church is the house of God?

∴ BIRTHDAY OF THE CHURCH ∴

We often call Pentecost the birthday of the Church. Have you considered the correlation between the events of that day and the day when the first Temple was dedicated? As Solomon stood before the people and finished praying his great prayer of dedication, there came from heaven what we often call the Shekinah glory of God. Fire fell from heaven and consumed the sacrifices and the glory of the presence of the Lord filled the temple. It was clear . . . God had come to His house!

On the day of Pentecost as the disciples gathered to pray, God once again dedicated His house. Again, fire fell from heaven. This time the fire didn't come to a building, but instead separated and came over the heads of the believers. A new temple was dedicated! And you are that temple. God's house is now His people, both when we are gathered in assemblies as well as individually. What hasn't changed is the name. God's house is still a house of prayer for all nations.

Can I press in on this a bit? It's too important to let go. There is much discussion and controversy today regarding the nature of the Church. Missional, emergent, post-Christian, simple church, post-modern . . . the list goes on in our attempt to define and describe the Church in these changing times. Where in the midst of the discussions are the leaders who are asking the Lord what He is calling His Church to be in these days?

Could it be that the answer is almost too simple? What if the Lord is saying to us today that we are trying too hard to figure out something that has already been set before us? Catch the beauty of this. The Father has named His house a house of prayer for all nations. When we grab hold of this, it transcends the changing of cultures. We are a praying people. Praying people who walk in intimacy with God will change whatever culture in which they find themselves.

It isn't that other issues are not important. They are. But when we line things up in God's order, everything else begins to fall into place. It's sort of like making sure you button your shirt from the top down, making sure you don't miss one button hole. Making the Church a house of prayer for all nations is buttoning your top button.

When it comes right down to it, it's not a matter for debate. The owner of the house get's to name the house. God has clearly, unequivocally named His house a house of prayer. Our job is to figure out what that means and do it!

.: POINTS TO PONDER :.

• If God clearly gave His house the name "House of Prayer," what does that mean for your church?

• Is your church a picture of that name?

• Where is prayer strong, and where is it weak in your fellowship?

• How can you better be a house of prayer?

CHAPTER TWO

·‖ ASKING WHY? ‖·

On the subject of being prepared and watchful for a coming revival, Theodore Cuyler writes,

"One day the wife of one of my two church elders came to me in my study, and told me that her son had been awakened by the faithful talk of a young Christian girl, who had brought some work to her husband's shoe store. I said to the elder's wife: 'The Holy Spirit is evidently working on one soul, let us have a prayer meeting at your house tonight.' We spent the afternoon in gathering our small congregation together, and when I got to her house it was packed to the door. I have attended thousands of prayer meetings since then, but never one that had a more distinct resemblance to the Pentecostal gathering in 'the upper room' at Jerusalem. The atmosphere seemed to be charged with a divine electricity that affected almost everyone in the house. Three times over I closed the meeting with a benediction, but it began again, and the people lingered until a very late hour, melted together by 'a baptism of fire.' That wonderful meeting was followed by special services every night, and the Holy Spirit descended with great power. My little church was doubled in numbers, and I learned more practical theology in a month than any seminary could teach me in a year.

"That revival was an illustration of the truth that a good work of grace often begins with the personal effort of one or two individuals. The Burlington awakening began with the little girl and the elder's wife. We ministers must never despise or neglect 'the day of small things.' Every pastor ought to be constantly on the watch, with open eyes and ears, for the first *signs of a special manifestation of the Spirit's presence. Elijah, on Carmel, did not only pray; he kept his eyes open to see the rising cloud. The moment that there is a manifestation of the Spirit's presence, it must be followed up promptly.*

"For example, during my pastorate in the Market Street Church, New York, (from 1853 to 1860), I was out one afternoon making calls, and I discovered that in two or three families there were anxious seekers for salvation. I immediately called for a series of meetings for almost every evening. A large ingathering of souls rewarded our efforts and prayers. I have no doubt that very often a spark of divine influence is allowed to die for want of being fanned by prayer and prompt labors, whereas, it is sometimes dashed out by inconsistent or quarrelsome church members. It was to Christians that St. Paul sent the message, 'Quench not the Spirit.'"

— *David Smithers,* The Pastor and Revival

ASKING WHY is often dangerous. Sometimes it doesn't seem like there is any good answer. Job asked why and got the greatest non-answer in history. Sometimes though, asking why will provide the foundation for further action. I believe that is the case regarding the Church being called a house of prayer for all nations. I hope the previous chapter convinced you that God has called us to be a house of prayer. Now I'd like to tackle the issue of why.

If we are going to line up with what God has called us to be, the issue of why is critical. I've spent more than 20 years traveling around this nation teaching that the Church is to be a house of prayer. To be honest, based on the tepid response, I would say that the greatest need is not for more practical tools to help us build prayer ministries, but for a solid theological basis for building houses of prayer. God has called us to be a house of prayer. Why? Why is prayer so important that the Lord would name His dwelling place a house of prayer?

.: SUPERNATURAL SIGNIFICANCE :.

It is important to recognize that we are dealing with something of supernatural significance here. The reaction of Jesus to the lack of prayer in the Temple is a huge clue that something is going on that perhaps many have not realized. The godly anger of Jesus could only be His response to something that is totally opposed to His and the Father's plan.

Mark's account of the cleansing of the Temple opens the door to a deeper understanding of this. In Mark 11:11 we read, "Jesus entered Jerusalem and went into the temple courts. He looked around at everything, but since it was already late, he went out to Bethany with the Twelve." The next day he came back with purpose, cleansing the Temple of the merchants who were defiling the place of prayer. Could it be that He and the Father had a long talk that night about what was happening in their house? Rather than a spur of the moment flare up, it was a carefully considered move that came about at the direction of the Father.

WE MADE PRAYER ABOUT US INSTEAD OF ABOUT GOD. WE LOOK TO PRAYER TO GET US WHAT WE WANT. PRAYER BECOMES OUR STRATEGY FOR GETTING THINGS FROM GOD.

God (Father, Son, and Spirit) has invested something of great significance in prayer. It is His way of bringing about change on planet earth and at the same time, bringing sons and daughters to maturity. Understanding both His purpose and His ways will not only change your perspective on prayer, but also on the purpose and nature of the Church.

It is important at the outset to stress that this plan is of God and is an outworking of His sovereignty. He is the omnipotent God and could have devised any plan to bring about His purposes on this planet. In His sovereignty and wisdom, He chose prayer as His strategy. He chose to give mankind a role to play in accomplishing His purposes as a means of helping us grow to maturity.

Instead, as we almost always do, we got it wrong. We made prayer about us instead of about God. We look to prayer to get us what we want. Prayer becomes our strategy for getting things from God. If we pray long enough, believe enough, gather enough others to join us, just maybe, we'll get what we want. We've turned prayer on its head and wonder why it doesn't work very well for us.

Prayer is from the beginning about God. All true prayer originates in the heart of the Father. When the Father wants something done, it is immediately known to the Spirit, "In the same way no one knows the thoughts of God except the Spirit of God" (1 Corinthians 2:11). Through the Spirit, God's will is made known to the believer. Then, through the name and authority of the Son, we pray back to the Father what He wanted to do in the first place. Mankind has a role . . . a vital role . . . but it's all about God! John Wesley said it this way, "God does nothing on earth save in answer to believing prayer."

My good friend and co-worker, Alvin VanderGriend developed the prayer cycle that illustrates this. The cycle puts the Father at the very top as the One who originates all true prayer. Then as you move clockwise at the 3:00 position is the place of the Spirit who takes from the Father and brings it to the believer. The believer is at the bottom position of the cycle. The believer receives from the Spirit what to pray, makes it his or her 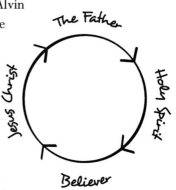 own, and then sends it on to the Father through Jesus. Jesus is at the 9:00 position. He takes the prayers of the believers and brings them on to the Father. VanderGriend often points out that there's only one weak link in the cycle and it isn't the Father, the Son, or the Spirit.

The Father is so amazing! He could have just done it Himself. But in His wisdom, He chose to bring us into the process through prayer, and through this, He trains us in spiritual matters. According to the Word of God, we are to reign with Christ as co-heirs (Romans 8:17). Years ago, Paul Billheimer in his classic, *Destined for the Throne*, said that prayer is on the job training for reigning with Christ.

When it comes right down to it, what do you do in this world that truly touches the spirit realm? It is prayer, through which we, who are both flesh and spirit, are trained in the area of the spirit. The Father is not going to short-circuit your training by intervening without you asking. "You do not have because you do not ask God" (James 4:2). And He is not going to give, until you spend the time in His Word and with Him to get to know His heart. It is then that we pray like Jesus taught us, "Your will be done, on earth as it is in heaven" (Matthew 6:10).

Martin Luther once said, "Prayer is not overcoming God's reluctance, but laying hold of His willingness."

One of the very best biblical examples of this truth is found in the Old Testament book of Ezekiel. The people of Judah and Jerusalem had continued to sin against the Lord and reject the word of the prophets. Finally, it was time for the consequences of sin to be poured out on the land. Yet, even then, the Lord desired for mercy to triumph over judgment. But for the Lord to do what He wanted, which was to show mercy, it would take someone to ask Him. God had decided to connect His work on earth with the prayers of His people.

"I looked for someone among them who would build up the wall and stand before me in the gap on behalf of the land so I would not have to destroy it, but I found no one" (Ezekiel 22:30). Whenever we find a verse of Scripture that tells us God is looking for someone, we should pay close attention. When the Creator of all things is looking for someone, it is very important!

This rich verse helps us understand the dealings of God with mankind, not just in this situation, but for all time. Unrepentant sin has consequences; in this case, the destruction of Jerusalem. But the verse also reveals the compassionate heart of the Father, showing that He is, even now, looking for ways to not destroy them. God has, however, tied His workings to the prayers of His people. So we find the all-powerful Creator, looking for an intercessor . . . someone who would stand in the gap and cry out on behalf of the land so that God might pour out His saving power. None are found, and the city is destroyed.

Please do not look at this truth about prayer as somehow limiting the power or the sovereignty of God. This is a self-imposed limit. God placed this limit on Himself so that His covenant people would accept responsibility and grow in spiritual maturity. It is no different than an earthly father who doesn't step in to provide something for his child, because the child has failed to ask properly. What we are seeing here is the amazing wisdom of God that transcends human understanding.

Another biblical example of this principle, with quite different results, is the story of Moses and the sin of the people of Israel. In Exodus

32, Israel turns against God and worships a golden calf. God determines to destroy them and tells Moses to get out of the way. But Moses intercedes. Israel is punished, but not destroyed. In Psalm 106:23, referring to that occasion, the Word says: "So he said he would destroy them—had not Moses, his chosen one, stood in the breach before him to keep his wrath from destroying them."

The words "breach" and "gap" are the same. In this situation, God found someone to stand in the gap (breach) and His mercy triumphed over judgment.

.: HIS WILL ON EARTH :.

Here is the heart of the matter, and that which should change the way we look at prayer forever: Prayer is the way God has chosen to accomplish His will on earth. When we understand that, suddenly prayer moves from something that can seem selfish and self-serving, to an amazing opportunity to be a participant in the work of God in our world.

PRAYER IS THE WAY GOD HAS CHOSEN TO ACCOMPLISH HIS WILL ON EARTH.

Now let's return to the Temple. Do you see why Jesus was so upset? It wasn't just a matter of some dishonest merchants. Jesus was surrounded by those in His culture. It was the perversion of the place of prayer. He and the Father had committed to prayer as the way they were going to work on the planet. The Temple was the heart of that plan, a house of prayer for all nations. In a real sense, the Temple was a picture for the world to see how God planned to operate on planet earth through the prayers of His people. If it wasn't going to be a place of prayer, there was no purpose for it at all.

Before the Temple, there was the tabernacle, and before that, the tent of meeting that Moses erected. All were intended to be places of prayer. In Exodus 33:7 and 11, we read of this amazing place of prayer: "Now Moses used to take a tent and pitch it outside the camp some distance away, calling it the 'tent of meeting.' Anyone inquiring of the LORD would go to the tent of meeting outside the camp. . . . The LORD would speak to Moses face to face, as one speaks to a friend."

For thousands of years now, the Lord has been trying to get a point across. Prayer is central to His purpose for and with His people. Martin Luther once said, "As is the business of tailors to make clothes and cobblers to make shoes, so it is the business of Christians to pray."

.: POINTS TO PONDER :.

• How does the concept of prayer originating with the Father change your view of prayer?

• How has prayer helped you grow in maturity as a follower of Jesus?

• What do you think would happen in your church if members really understood the purpose of prayer?

• Who is "standing in the gap" for your church?

CHAPTER THREE

··∥ JESUS AND PRAYER ∥··

J. O. Peck was a respected and successful Methodist pastor in the latter part of the 19th century. He had been both a witness and an instrument of many genuine revivals. From his own experience he had learned that, "In every revival there is an inter-blending of the divine and the human agencies." Therefore he regularly warned the Church against neglecting their duty to pray for revival. Some have falsely assumed that because a revival seemingly comes without noticeable preparation and prayer, that such things are not necessary.

Addressing this subject Mr. Peck writes, "There are times when revivals seem to be spontaneous manifestations of divine power, having no visible human agency at work. Dr. Lyman Beecher had one of these spontaneous revivals. It came suddenly and powerfully. It swept the town with mighty power. After it was over Dr. Beecher was visiting a bedridden member of his church in a remote part of the town. This member told him that day after day for weeks he had felt a great burden of prayer for the unsaved, and that he began at one end of the town and prayed for each household till he had included every family. Then, as if this were not enough, he prayed for each family again. In an instant Dr. Beecher knew from whence the revival came. It was born in the heart of that bedridden mighty wrestler with God!"

— David Smithers, The Pastor and Revival *(From awakeandgo.com)*

IF WE ARE GOING to dig deep and truly understand prayer, we are going to have to examine the prayer life of Jesus and all that He taught on the subject. Jesus has a unique perspective on prayer. He is the only one who understands prayer from both sides. He prays to His Father, and on the other hand, as God, He is prayed to. He certainly has something to say to us about this subject.

Even a cursory reading of the Gospels shows us the priority Jesus gave to prayer in His own life. Consider these occurrences:

Matthew 4:1-11—40 days of fasting in the desert.

Mark 1:35—"Very early in the morning, while it was still dark, Jesus got up, left the house and went off to a solitary place, where he prayed."

Luke 5:16—"But Jesus often withdrew to lonely places and prayed."

Luke 6:12-13—"One of those days Jesus went out to a mountainside to pray, and spent the night praying to God. When morning came, he called his disciples to him and chose twelve of them, whom he also designated apostles."

Mark 6:46—"After leaving them, he went up on a mountainside to pray."

Luke 9:28—"About eight days after Jesus said this, he took Peter, John, and James with him and up onto a mountain to pray."

Luke 10:21-22—Jesus prayed after the return of the 72.

Matthew 11:25-27—Praise to the Father

Matthew 14:23—"After he had dismissed them, he went up on a mountain by himself to pray."

John 17:1-26—The entire chapter is Jesus' prayer.

Luke 22:41-44—Praying in Gethsemane

Luke 23:34—Praying from the cross

.: WHY HE PRAYED :.

It is important for us to consider why Jesus prayed. All too often I hear people say that Jesus prayed as an example for us. While He is certainly a good example of a praying man, His prayer life goes way beyond that. If He was praying merely as an example, He would not have made so many attempts to withdraw from others and pray in secret. No, Jesus prayed not just as a model, but because He had to pray.

Psalm 2:7-8 gives us insight into the "why" of the prayer life of Jesus. In this amazing passage, we are privileged to hear a conversation between the Father and the Son. "[The Father] said to me, 'You are my Son; today I have become your Father. Ask me, and I will make the nations your inheritance, the ends of the earth your possession.'"

The Father promises to give the Son "the nations" for His willingness to take on human flesh and fulfill the plan of redemption. But, because Jesus is also fully human, He is under the constraints of God's plan for giving to us. You do not have because you do not ask. Even Jesus, as the Son of Man, had to ask in order to receive. Prayer is the key for human participation in the works of God.

Prayer was an essential part of the ministry of Jesus. That makes perfect sense since it was His and His Father's plan to get things done on this planet through prayer. Jesus often withdrew to quiet places to be alone with His Father and to understand what He must do. Jesus said of Himself, "the Son can do nothing by himself; he can do only what he sees his Father doing" (John 5:19). Jesus models the essential aspect of intimacy with God in prayer.

PRAYER IS THE KEY FOR HUMAN PARTICIPATION IN THE WORKS OF GOD.

The personal prayer life of Jesus was so central to His ministry and so obvious that it led His disciples to ask Him to teach them to pray (Luke 11). It is fascinating to note that nowhere in Scripture is it recorded that the disciples asked Jesus to teach them anything other than prayer. They watched the amazing life and ministry of Jesus and correctly made the connection to His prayer life. If they were to follow Jesus, they needed to learn to pray like Jesus.

So much has been written about what we often call the Lord's

Prayer that I hesitate to add anything. I would simply suggest that this model prayer is God-centered and kingdom-focused. Jesus certainly gives us permission in it to pray about personal matters such as daily bread and dealing with temptation. As I pray the Lord's Prayer, I often get the feeling that after I have worshiped the Holy One and have poured myself into praying for the kingdom to come on earth as it is in heaven, that whatever bit of energy or time I have left is for personal issues. Jesus teaches us to focus on His Father's agenda in prayer.

Some of the most difficult teachings of Jesus on prayer are found in the Gospel of John in chapters 14-16. If it were possible, it almost sounds as though Jesus over-promises.

> **John 14:13**—"And I will do whatever you ask in my name, so that the Father may be glorified in the Son."
>
> **John 14:14**—"You may ask me for anything in my name, and I will do it."
>
> **John 15:7**—"If you remain in me and my words remain in you, ask whatever you wish, and it will be done for you."
>
> **John 15:16**—"Whatever you ask in my name the Father will give you."
>
> **John 16:23**—"I tell you, the Father will give you whatever you ask in my name."
>
> **John 16:24**—"Until now you have not asked for anything in my name. Ask and you will receive, and your joy will be complete."

There is a tendency to try to spiritualize these teachings away. Or to simply believe that Jesus was talking in generalities. But what if Jesus meant exactly what He said. "Ask me for anything in my name and I will do it." If prayer is that which begins with God and is all about accomplishing His agenda on earth, then suddenly these promises seem very practical and do-able. The prayer promises of Jesus are not invitations to selfishness, but to participation in the divine plan.

Ultimately then, these promises have to do more with relationship than our desire to receive something in prayer. In this same section of Scripture, Jesus teaches us that He is the vine and that we are the branches. We are not separate, but connected. The only thing that flows through the branches are the things that originate in the vine. When we remain in Him, then the things that are in Him, that He desires, become possible for us when we ask.

PRAYER FOR US BECOMES THAT CONNECTEDNESS THROUGH THE SPIRIT WITH THE FATHER AND SON, SO THAT WHAT THEY DESIRE MIGHT BE ACCOMPLISHED ON EARTH THROUGH THE PRAYING CHRISTIAN.

It's really the same for us as it was for Jesus in His fleshly form. He said that He only did those things He saw His Father doing. The things He said were the things He heard the Father saying. Prayer for us becomes that connectedness through the Spirit with the Father and Son, so that what they desire might be accomplished on earth through the praying Christian. "On earth as it is in heaven."

There is much more that Jesus taught on prayer. It is pervasive throughout His teachings. A few samplings include:

Luke 18:1-7–We should always pray and not give up.

Luke 11:1-13–Teachings on prayer including Lord's Prayer, a parable of friend at midnight, and how much more the Father will give to us than we give to our children.

Matthew 6:5-15–Sermon on the mount, focusing on motives for prayer.

Matthew 7:7-12–Ask, seek, knock.

Matthew 9:37-38–Ask the Lord of the harvest for workers for the harvest.

It becomes evident that prayer for Jesus was not a side issue. It was not just a good spiritual exercise. Nor was it something you do when nothing else works. Prayer was central to who He was and what He did.

He was going to pray, as well as teach His disciples to pray, throughout His ministry. And His final words from the cross would be a prayer!

E.M. Bounds reminds us that "we can do nothing without prayer. All things can be done by importunate prayer. That is the teaching of Jesus Christ."

.: POINTS TO PONDER :.

• Why do you believe Jesus prayed?

• How would prayer change in your church if we prayed as Jesus prayed?

• If we asked Jesus to teach us to pray as the disciples did, what do you think would happen?

• How have you dealt with the amazing promises of Jesus regarding prayer, versus what actually happens when you pray?

CHAPTER FOUR

·◦‖ THE DANGERS OF A PRAYERLESS CHURCH ‖◦·

We are in the infancy stage of planting our church, The Agora Community, in Rochester, NY. With everything so new, there are many things that need to happen. I often attack projects head on, and with my head down. However, my coach, J.R. Briggs, uses a phrase that has stuck with me over the course of this season: "If this is your church, you better hurry up and start. If this is Jesus' church, you better slow down and listen." When you plant a church, you begin to realize how little you have to bring to the table. If this thing is to be fruitful, it will be because God is moving.

I had been given a number of a person in the area who might be interested in what we're doing. I generally don't like cold calling people as a first point of contact, so while I took the number, I sat on it for awhile. A week later, I was walking a path in the town we are starting the church, and praying for how we could break into the community. I was alone and felt comfortable praying out loud. As I prayed, a jogger snuck up behind me and certainly heard me "talking to myself." While I felt funny, in that exchange I also felt the Lord telling me that I needed to call this guy I had been putting off. Right there on the path I gave him a call. I left him a message and waited for a call back. A few hours later he responded and told me he owns a percussion shop in town and invited me to come by to talk. As soon as I walked into the store we both recognized each other. He was the jogger on the path. What followed was a conversation about a small group of people who were gathering at his home to explore what a fresh expression of church might look like in their community. This group had formed at the beginning of the summer and had been sensing that they needed direction. Just that morning he had been praying to provide the next step for the group—then he got my call. The result has been a weekly Sunday gathering as we are praying, worshiping, and discussing the potential of joining together. God is moving.

— Bryan Long, Angora Community, from ecclesianet.org, fall 2012

EVERY CHURCH has members who pray. But that doesn't make it a praying church. For all too many local congregations, prayer is an assumed value and practice. Bad assumption!

The first place to look to see if a church is a praying church is to look at its prayer meetings. Many churches have no regular prayer meetings at all. Those that do have prayer meetings typically report that they are very poorly attended. If we are not coming together for the purpose of prayer, can we in any way be regarded as a praying church?

Individually we don't do much better. Most surveys indicate that the average American Christian prays three minutes or less a day. Pastors are twice as good. That's right. In at least some polls, pastors are only praying six minutes a day on average. That's moving a long way from the apostolic practice in Acts 6 in which they declared that they had given themselves to prayer and the ministry of the Word.

If you want to do a quick self-evaluation of how your church is doing in prayer, there are several areas to examine. Look at your calendar. Important things in your congregational life are on the calendar. If prayer isn't there, it isn't important for your church. Look at your building. Is there a prayer room that has any use? Are provisions for prayer made in your worship center? Like it or not, your building says much about your priorities. Then look at your budget. Is there a line item for prayer? Your budget speaks volumes about your congregational priorities. If you aren't spending money on something, it doesn't have a high value to your church.

.: NOT WORRIED :.

I don't think I have to work too hard to make the case that the Church in America is not as a whole, a praying Church. In more than two decades of traveling extensively in churches, almost no church leaders have told me that they feel their congregation is doing well in prayer. What is perhaps more alarming, however, is this fact doesn't seem to worry them. While almost all Christian leaders are for prayer, most are not about it! Author Paul Billheimer says it well, "A church without an intelligent, well-organized, and systematic prayer program is simply operating a religious treadmill."

There are some inherent dangers in being a prayerless church. Those who are shepherds of their flocks should always be on the lookout for danger. While many are on the watch (correctly) for the dangers of false doctrine, divisiveness, or immorality, a more subtle, yet perhaps more damaging danger has set up camp: prayerlessness. A church that is not given to prayer is an affront to the Lord.

The chief danger of prayerlessness is pride. When prayer is not front and center, we can begin to feel that whatever is happening that is good in our congregation is the result of our hard work, or great ideas, or fantastic marketing. We so easily forget the words of Jesus in John 15:5, "apart from me you can do nothing." Failing to pray is failing to trust in the Lord and in His strength.

Ronnie Floyd in his great book, *How to Pray*, makes this profound statement:

1. Prayer occurs when you depend on God.

2. Prayerlessness occurs when you depend on yourself.

When prayer is used simply to open and close meetings, we are walking in the pride that says, "We can do this ourselves, Lord. We'll let You know if we need anything." A praying church is a church that has turned from pride and is walking in humility before the Lord.

In a very real sense, all of the other dangers of prayerlessness in the Church emerge from this sin of pride. For instance, there is the danger of being unconnected to our Head, the Lord Jesus. We believe according to the Word of God that Jesus is Head of the

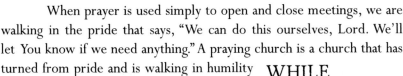

WHILE ALMOST ALL CHRISTIAN LEADERS ARE FOR PRAYER, MOST ARE NOT ABOUT IT!

Church. Paul wrote to the Ephesians: "speaking the truth in love, we will grow to become in every respect the mature body of him who is the head, that is, Christ" (Ephesians 4:15). How do we stay connected to our Head if not through prayer? A Church that is not regularly praying is a Church that is not connected well with its Head, which means it is not moving in accord with the One who is in charge. As my friend David Bryant often says, "We have made Jesus our mascot, instead of our monarch."

This lack of connectivity leads to a failure to receive direction from our Leader. So many congregations are more about elections and lining up support, than about seeking the heart of God and finding out the direction the Lord would have us go. Rather than spending the time in prayer and allowing our Leader to show us what to do, we adopt the methods of corporate America to develop our strategic plans. Opening your meeting with prayer is not the same as seeking the face of God!

.: THE WATERMARK OF OWNERSHIP :.

Do we really believe that the Church is the Bride of Christ? That we belong to Him? Prayer becomes the watermark of ownership and intimacy. It is in prayer that we quit simply talking about Jesus and begin to talk to Him. It is in prayer that we begin to practice what it means for Christ to truly be Head of the Church.

I love the way Indian pastor Sadhu Sundar Singh focuses on the essence of relationship in prayer.

The essence of prayer does not consist in asking God for something but in opening our hearts to God, in speaking with Him, and living with Him in perpetual communion. Prayer is continual abandonment to God. Prayer does not mean asking God for all kinds of things we want; it is rather the desire for God Himself, the only Giver of Life. Prayer is not asking, but union with God. Prayer is not a painful effort to gain from God help in the varying needs of our lives. Prayer is the desire to possess God Himself, the Source of all life. The true spirit of prayer does not consist in asking for blessings, but in receiving

Him who is the Giver of all blessings, and in living a life of
fellowship with Him. *(awakeandgo.com)*

Think about the way many churches go about finding pastors. Rather than fasting and praying, there are resumes and search committees. We make up the list of qualities that we want and then go looking for the person to fit our list. How often we miss that divine connection between man of God and congregation! Can you imagine a congregation accepting Moses, as he was at the beginning of his leadership ministry? He's 80 years old and stutters. Or Paul, a former persecutor of Christians who wasn't a gifted speaker, and counseled his student Timothy to take a little wine for his stomach problems. The list could go on, couldn't it? We miss God's best when we do not make prayer a priority in our churches.

Perhaps the most obvious danger of prayerlessness is the lack of real power in the Church today. We speak of power and sing of power and yet see so very little power in our lives. The source of spiritual power is, of course, God. But that power will not be realized in our lives apart from the amazing connection to God called prayer. It is prayer that provides the channel through which the power of God runs into and through our lives.

I love this statement from S.D. Gordon on the power of prayer:

The great people of the earth today are the people who pray! I do not mean those who talk about prayer; nor those who say they believe in prayer; nor those who explain prayer; but I mean those who actually take the time to pray. They have not time. It must be taken from something else. That something else is important, very important and pressing, but still, less important and pressing than prayer. There are people who put prayer first, and group the other items in life's schedule around and after prayer. These are the people today who are doing the most for God in winning souls, in solving problems, in awakening churches, in supplying both men and money for mission posts, in keeping fresh and strong their lives far off in sacrificial service on the foreign field, where the thickest fighting is going on, and in keeping the old earth sweet a little while longer. *(Quiet Talks on Prayer, p. 5)*

I do not doubt that there is still spiritual power in the Church today. Lives are being transformed by the preaching of the gospel. The Church is still being used by God today to make a difference. But, there is so much more that could be happening! When we look at the first believers in Jerusalem, the difference in levels of power is obvious. It comes down to a biblical principle written by the James, the brother of Jesus: "You do not have because you do not ask God" (James 4:2).

As we move toward the end of the age, the Church must face the fact that it is only through the power of God that we will be able to stand against the onslaught of ungodliness that will come against us. As important as our words are, by themselves they are and will be insufficient.

IT IS ONLY THROUGH THE POWER OF GOD THAT WE WILL BE ABLE TO STAND AGAINST THE ONSLAUGHT OF UNGODLINESS THAT WILL COME AGAINST US.

The Apostle Paul was very concerned that those who heard him would not just hear words, but see the power of God at work. "My message and my preaching were not with wise and persuasive words, but with a demonstration of the Spirit's power" (1 Corinthians 2:4).

When the Church begins to pray, we will once again see that demonstration of the Spirit's power. E.M. Bounds concurs: "God shapes the world by prayer. The more prayer there is in the world, the better the world will be, the mightier the forces against evil."

.: POINTS TO PONDER :.

• How would you evaluate the prayer life of your church?

• Are you seeing the effects of prayerlessness or powerful prayer in your church? How?

• What do you believe would happen if you surveyed your members regarding their personal prayer lives?

• How would your congregation respond to bringing large amounts of prayer into your regular times of worship?

CHAPTER FIVE

··⫼ THE EARLY CHURCH ⫼··

Nearly 200 people have come to faith in Christ since Hope Church started, and most are being discipled. On Easter Sunday 2012, we had almost 1,200 people in four services. God has continued to do amazing things, including physical healings, financial provisions, and spiritual deliverance. These things have not happened because I'm strong; I'm weak. It's because the Lord is on the move in our community. We have no specific goals. We have no contemporary strategies. We have no long-range plans. We just pray that the Lord of the harvest will stretch forth His hand and bring hungry people to Himself. And every week, people drive past the building, stop, come in, and find Jesus. People visit our prayer meeting regularly, and we have many new families every Sunday.

When God says that He wants us to ask, He means it. After 30 years of ministry and participating in multiple prayer summits, I've never seen God miraculously answer prayer like He has in the past three years. To see the Lord at work has been a tremendous blessing.

We don't have a lot of fancy programs at Hope Church, and we don't have it all together. We're just simple people who trust God, believing that "if two of you on earth agree about anything you ask for, it will be done for you by my Father in heaven" (Matt. 18:19). This has been the most exhilarating, stretching, humbling experience I've ever had.

—Gordon Meier, "When Jesus Is All You Have,"
Issue 6, Prayer Connect *magazine*

I GREW UP in church that was a part of a fellowship of churches that emphasized restoring New Testament Christianity. That meant the book of Acts was huge for us! We really wanted to see what apostolic Christianity looked like and emulate it as closely as possible. We succeeded in some areas and missed it in several areas.

One of the areas we missed was prayer. The New Testament Church was a praying fellowship. When I am teaching on the nature and practice of the Church in congregations, I love to give them the assignment of going home and re-reading the book of Acts. As they read, I want them to ask the question: "What did the early Church do when it met together?" It's not difficult to see. They prayed! More than preaching, teaching, worship, or anything else, what the Bible shows is a group of people who came together to spend time talking with their Resurrected Lord.

Armin Gesswein in his wonderful book, *With One Accord in One Place*, wrote of this,

> When Jesus builds His church, He builds a praying congregation. Every single member was a praying member. A strong praying member. An intercessor. A real priest. In this Jerusalem congregation we do not read of a "church within the church" (ecclesiola in ecclesia, as it is called). All the members were together. All were "with one accord in one place."
>
> Nor do we read of "the church prayer meeting," as today. The church was the prayer meeting. The entire assembly was at prayer." (p. 20)

Consider the central role of prayer in the life of the earliest believers in the book of Acts:

Acts 1:14—"They all joined together constantly in prayer."

Acts 2:42—"They devoted themselves to the apostles' teaching and to fellowship, to the breaking of bread and to prayer."

Acts 3:1—"One day Peter and John were going up to the temple at the time of prayer."

Acts 4:24–"When they heard this, they raised their voices together in prayer to God."

Acts 4:31–"After they prayed, the place where they were meeting was shaken."

Acts 6:4–"[We] will give our attention to prayer and the ministry of the word."

Acts 6:6–"They presented these men to the apostles, who prayed and laid their hands on them."

Acts 7:59–"While they were stoning him, Stephen prayed."

Acts 9:11–"The Lord told him, 'Go to the house of Judas on Straight Street and ask for a man from Tarsus named Saul, for he is praying.'"

Acts 9:40–"Peter sent them all out of the room; then he got down on his knees and prayed."

Acts 10:9–"About noon ... Peter went up on the roof to pray."

Acts 12:5–"So Peter was kept in prison, but the church was earnestly praying to God for him."

Acts 12:12–"He went to the house of Mary, the mother of John, also called Mark, where many people had gathered and were praying."

Acts 13:2–"While they were worshiping the Lord and fasting . . ."

Acts 14:23–"Paul and Barnabas appointed elders for them in each church and, with prayer and fasting, committed them to the Lord."

Acts 16:16–"Once when we were going to the place of prayer . . ."

Acts 16:25–"About midnight Paul and Silas were praying and singing hymns to God . . ."

Acts 20:36–"When Paul had finished speaking, he knelt down with all of them and prayed."

Acts 21:5–". . . and there on the beach we knelt to pray."

Acts 28:8–"Paul went in to see him and, after prayer, placed his hands on him and healed him."

.: NOT WINDOW DRESSING :.

Prayer in Acts was obviously not window-dressing. It was not just a way to open or close meetings. It was a part of everything they did. And the power of God was poured out in amazing ways in response to their prayers. What congregation would not want to see this happen in its midst? If we want to see power, we must see prayer.

One of the most significant practical aspects of prayer in Acts is the way it impacted and led their decisions. It could be argued that virtually every major decision made by the Church was made at a prayer meeting. In Acts 1, the prayer meeting was interrupted to choose a new apostle. Acts 10 features the door of salvation opening to the Gentiles as Peter prays on a rooftop. In Acts 13, a new missions strategy was born out of a time of worship and fasting.

TO BE A CHRIST-CENTERED, SPIRIT-LED CHURCH WILL MEAN SEEKING THE LORD IN PRAYER, RATHER THAN TRUSTING IN OUR OWN DEVICES.

The difference in these situations, and the typical decision-making process in today's church, has to do with intent. These early believers were coming together to pray and seek the Lord. In the midst of that time, a decision was made . . . a new direction was laid out for them. We today often come together for the purposes of making decisions, with prayer added in. It's a matter of intent. To be a Christ-centered, Spirit-led Church will mean seeking the Lord in prayer, rather than trusting in our own devices.

Prayer had a strategic role in the early Church. Much of the ministry that was accomplished seemed tied to their prayers. So often, whether it was setting apart deacons for a new work, or healing the sick, you see in Scripture that they prayed, and then laid on hands that ministered in the power of God. Prayer was a very practical part of how they served the Lord and one another. They understood that for ministry to be lasting, it must be birthed in prayer.

One of the most fascinating passages in Acts is found in Chapter 4, verses 23-31. Here we actually get to read a prayer prayed during a time of corporate prayer. Peter and John had just been arrested by the Sanhedrin and the Church gathered to pray for their release. After being ordered not to speak any more in Jesus name, Peter and John are released and come to the home where the Church was praying. The response of those gathered is this astonishing prayer:

"On their release, Peter and John went back to their own people and reported all that the chief priests and the elders had said to them. When they heard this, they raised their voices together in prayer to God. "Sovereign Lord," they said, "you made the heavens and the earth and the sea, and everything in them. You spoke by the Holy Spirit through the mouth of your servant, our father David:

" 'Why do the nations rage
        and the peoples plot in vain?
The kings of the earth rise up
        and the rulers band together
against the Lord
        and against his anointed one.

"Indeed Herod and Pontius Pilate met together with the Gentiles and the people of Israel in this city to conspire against your holy servant Jesus, whom you anointed. They did what your power and will had decided beforehand should happen. Now, Lord, consider their threats and enable your servants to speak your word with great boldness. Stretch out your hand to heal and perform signs and wonders through the name of your holy servant Jesus."

After they prayed, the place where they were meeting was

shaken. And they were all filled with the Holy Spirit and spoke the word of God boldly." (Acts 4:23-31)

It's almost as though someone was sitting in the corner taking notes on the prayer meeting. This is a prayer of great boldness. They begin their prayer by focusing on the Creator. Then they base their prayer on Scripture, using Psalm 2 as the foundation for their requests. They pray a big prayer that focuses on the gospel going to all nations, regardless of the opposition of the authorities. How different than most of our prayer meetings! What would happen if we began to pray like they prayed?

If we are to see New Testament power in our churches, we must have New Testament prayer. It is prayer that is pervasive and prevailing. Prayer that is intense and intentional. Not relegated to a few specialists, it is for the whole Church. New Testament Christians were praying Christians!

Once again, let me defer to Armin Gesswein:

> I have read portions of the book of Acts hundreds of times and some portions more than a thousand times. Finally it hit me: What is the story of this Jerusalem church? It is the story of one small praying congregation of about 120 members in an upper room in the city of Jerusalem which got on fire for God and went on to change the world!
>
> That says it! What a revealing and revolutionary discovery!
>
> If you were to ask me what is the greatest discovery I have made regarding the truth of the church, I would have to say it is this: When Jesus built the church, He built a praying congregation! (*With One Accord in One Place*, pp. 21-22)

As I read the book of Acts, I am encouraged that they were not a perfect Church. If they were perfect, I would not even try to be like them. But Scripture presents the early Church, with all its flaws, as a group of praying people who followed Jesus in the power of the Holy Spirit. As they trusted the Lord to work through them as they prayed, they changed the world around them. The same promise is before a praying Church today!

.: POINTS TO PONDER :.

• Were you surprised at the tremendous attention given to prayer in the book of Acts? How so?

• How can you bring more prayer into the decision-making process of your church?

• As you look at the praying church in Acts, how would you compare that with the prayer in your church?

• How would the ministries of your church be impacted if prayer was central?

CHAPTER 6

·╫ BUILDING PRAYING LEADERS ╫·

Not long ago, I was in a church that clearly "gets it" where prayer is concerned. Mountain View Community Church in Fresno, CA, hosted our "Can Prayer Save America?" event this past February. From the time the conference opened, it was evident that prayer is simply a part of this church's DNA.

When we lead such a conference, we ask that the host church provide worship. We did not coach the worship team at Mountain View to lead in a certain way, yet the worship experience was loaded with prayer. Multiple times the worship leader prayed in between songs. His song selections were clearly related to the theme—crying out for God to send revival and spiritual awakening.

Several times during a worship song, Mountain View people approached a microphone and prayed, reflecting the song's content. At one point during a particular song, the main prayer leader asked people from the audience to pray bold, transforming truths related to revival and awakening. It was a powerful moment.

But this church wasn't just putting prayer front and center because it was a prayer conference. Prayer permeates its ministry each Sunday and throughout the week. Pastor Fred Leonard models prayer and disciples his staff to engage in prayer. They all keep prayer / spiritual growth journals— and for accountability, they must regularly share from their journals during staff meetings. Their weekly two- to three-hour staff meetings are characterized by an hour to even half of their meeting time, given to praying together.

In Sunday school and small groups church leaders provide regular training regarding prayer. Every year they schedule at least two prayer initiatives—from a week to 40 days—during which the entire congregation is praying on the same theme. Mountain View wants every congregant to be discipled in prayer so that he or she knows how to pray with confidence. The leadership does not leave it to chance!

The most intriguing thing that sets them apart from every other church I know: Anyone who steps into leadership (such as elders, small group leaders, and those in teaching roles) must take a 12-week "prayer usher" class before they are qualified—and then they must receive ongoing prayer training.

A prayer usher (a term coined by Dr. Terry Teykl) is trained in taking individuals and their issues before God's throne of grace. They usher people—through praying for and with them—into God's presence. These trained ushers are the ones who pray with people at the altar, visit the sick, or encourage those in need of ministry support. The church also trains prayer ushers who are not directly involved in other leadership.

Finally, Mountain View demonstrates a regional prayer influence by encouraging Fresno churches to pray together. Now a significant number of churches participate in a yearly prayer calendar that includes ten joint prayer events. Pastors pray together, within geographic clusters, weekly or monthly around the city.

—Jonathan Graf, "As Natural as Breathing," Prayer Connect, Issue 4

IF YOU'VE SERVED any length of time in any Christian congregation, you know what it is to deal with complaining saints. It's one of the sad realities of church life. Lest we think its a modern phenomenon, just look at Acts 6:1 "...the Hellenistic Jews among them complained against the Hebraic Jews because their widows were being overlooked in the daily distribution of food." Complaining Christians have a long lineage!

It's fascinating to see how the leaders of the church in Jerusalem dealt with the situation that created complaining. It certainly would have been easy for them to step up and handle the unequal distribution of food to widows themselves. But they didn't. They asked the church to choose other qualified leaders to handle this situation. Why didn't they do it themselves? Because they had a prior commitment. "We will . . . give our attention to prayer and the ministry of the word" (Acts 6:4).

One of the key marks of spiritual leadership is knowing your calling and priorities. The apostles had those marks. They knew that heaven's calling to them was for prayer and the ministry of the Word. It wasn't that other things were not important or necessary. It's just that they needed to make sure that prayer and the ministry of the Word was given the priority.

My friend, Daniel Henderson, often says that when he graduated from seminary, he came out with his sword sharpened on one side. We often train our leaders in the ministry of the Word, but neglect the ministry of prayer. A sword sharpened on just one side is not as sharp or effective as one sharpened on both sides. I believe that is a good description of much of leadership ministry today.

It's not that Christian leaders today are against prayer. That's just not so. But prayer is not necessarily high on their priority list, especially when you gauge it against the other things that compete for their time. At least part of the reason for this is they have not been trained in prayer for their personal life nor in leading a church to become a praying church. How did it come about that so few pastors feel equipped in leading in prayer?

In the next chapter, we'll discuss in greater depth the role of spiritual warfare in our prayerlessness, but I'd like to address one specific issue relating to that here. Most of what we deal with in spiritual warfare is what I call micro level. That's personal temptations and issues we face regularly. But there is also macro level warfare that moves to a higher level. It is on that macro level that I believe Satan won a great victory many centuries ago.

.: SATAN'S VICTORY :.

Somewhere along the line, hundreds of years ago, Satan convinced good, godly scholars that prayer was not a topic worthy of academic study. I can almost hear the thoughts diabolically placed in their minds: "Of course prayer is important. But we can't expect it to be relegated to a classroom. Our students should just pray." It sounds true doesn't it? There's just enough truth to be deadly.

Through the years, prayer has become completely experiential, with little to no serious theological thought given to it. Look at the books that seminarians have studied called "systematic theologies." You will find the study of salvation (soteriology), the church (ecclesiology), second coming (eschatology) and many other ologies. But you won't find prayer.

Here's the problem with that. A theology of a topic requires that you think deeply about the area. It will push a student to delve into it and examine it from every area. Because we have not done that with prayer, we have the common situation where pastors believe that prayer is important, but they aren't sure why. If an area of the Christian life has not been studied in the academic setting, it will often take a backseat when it comes to actual practice.

Of course, there is always the danger of making prayer merely an academic topic for study instead of a dynamic encounter with Jesus Christ. But we have clearly allowed the pendulum to swing the other way and have

SEMINARIES AND BIBLE COLLEGES MUST BECOME LABORATORIES FOR DYNAMIC PRAYER MINISTRY.

ignored the opportunities to train our pastors and church leaders in powerful personal prayer and what could happen when they lead their congregations to become a praying people.

Seminaries and Bible colleges must become laboratories for dynamic prayer ministry. A few years ago, America's National Prayer Committee looked at the current situation and moved to commission a textbook on prayer for use in our schools. *Giving Ourselves to Prayer: An Acts 6:4 Primer for Ministry* is increasingly being used as seminaries become aware of this deficiency in pastoral preparedness. More than a textbook is needed though. Some brave academicians will need to fight the curriculum wars to bring a serious study of prayer to become required training for pastors.

It isn't only at the level of training however that this battle must be fought. Christian leaders will need to educate the local church of the need for praying leaders. One of the saddest illustrations I know comes from a church in the Midwest that told their pastor, "You work on our time. You pray on your own time." What grief that perspective must bring to the Lord! Contrast that to Andrew Murray's comment: "Time spent in prayer will yield more than that given to work. Prayer alone gives work its worth and its success. Prayer opens the way for God Himself to do His work in us and through us. Let our chief work as God's messengers be intercession; in it we secure the presence and power of God to go with us."

Countless generations have failed to see the spiritual work of prayer in the church. Prayer has been a tool to call meetings to order, and has been seen as the work of a few spiritual giants. We don't necessarily expect or even want our pastors to be people of prayer. If you disagree, then look over the job descriptions of most congregations when looking for a pastor. Prayer is often completely missing! Rarely does a church ask a candidating pastor, "Tell us about your prayer life."

It will not be easy to turn this ship around. It will take godly, visionary leaders at all levels to see this happen. From seminaries and Bible colleges to pastors and congregational leaders, all will need to stand together to say, "This must change! We must give ourselves to prayer and the ministry of the Word!"

Many of the greatest leaders of the Church through the years have testified to the critical need of prayer for those in leadership. See if these words stir you as they have me:

 "I would rather teach one man to pray than ten men to preach."
–Charles H. Spurgeon

"Prayer is my chief work, and it is by means of it that I carry on the rest." –Thomas Hooker, Puritan

"[The] power of prayer can never be overrated. They who cannot serve God by preaching need not regret. If a man can but pray he can do anything. He who knows how to overcome with God in prayer has Heaven and earth at his disposal."
–Charles H. Spurgeon

"What the church needs today is not more machinery or better, not new organizations or more novel methods, but men whom the Holy Ghost can use–men of prayer, men mighty in prayer."
–E.M. Bounds

"Ministers who do not spend two hours a day in prayer are not worth a dime a dozen–degrees or no degrees." –Leonard Ravenhill

"Out of a very intimate acquaintance with D. L. Moody, I wish to testify that he was a far greater pray–er than he was preacher. Time and time again, he was confronted by obstacles that seemed insurmountable, but he always knew the way to overcome all difficulties. He knew the way to bring to pass anything that needed to be brought to pass. He knew and believed in the deepest depths of his soul that nothing was too hard for the Lord, and that prayer could do anything that God could do." –R. A. Torrey

.: POINTS TO PONDER :.

• How committed to prayer are the leaders of your church?

• Were you surprised to hear of the lack of training in prayer in Bible colleges and seminaries? Why or why not?

• What do you believe can be done to restore a proper understanding of the role of prayer in spiritual leadership?

• Are there steps your church can take to make prayer a prerequisite for leadership?

CHAPTER 7

··ǁ THE WAR ON PRAYER ǁ··

While it is true that we finite creatures cannot predict the [exact] times or seasons of the Spirit's special presence, yet it is always right to be praying for an outpouring of the power from on high. The late Dr. Thos. H. Skinner told me that two or three of his elders, in Philadelphia, met in his study to prostrate themselves before God, and to ask for a baptism of the Spirit. They emptied themselves and prayed to be filled with Christ. He did fill them. Then they interceded most fervently for the awakening and conversion of sinners. Presently a most powerful revival shook the whole church like the mighty blast which filled the upper room at Pentecost. Mr. Finney tells us that for fourteen successive winters there was a rich spiritual blessing brought down upon a certain church just because it was the custom of the church officers to "Pray fervently for their minister far into the night before each Sabbath." Those wise, godly men honored Christ's ambassador, honored His gospel, honored their own duty and felt their own responsibility. They did not run off to Egypt for help. The prayer-hearing God honored them . . . When the influences of the Spirit are recognized in your congregation in any degree, you must be on the alert, and be prompt and untiring in your cooperation with the Divine Agent. The secret of success in a revival is to cooperate with the Holy Spirit.

—Theodore Cuyler, Cooperating with the Spirit, *from* Pastors and Revival, *by David Smithers*

YOU KNOW of course, that our enemy hates prayer. He will let you do anything rather than pray. That point was driven home for me some years ago after I returned from a prayer conference, determined to get up early each day to pray. I set the alarm for 5:30 am. I got up and prepared myself for prayer. I had no sooner begun to pray when suddenly I had this overwhelming desire to wash my car. Wash my car? At 5:30 in the morning? Where could such an outlandish thought come from? I don't like to wash my car ever, much less at 5:30 in the morning.

Satan will do whatever he can to distract us away from the one thing that can defeat him. That morning in my room, I realized that the thought of washing my car was not my own . . . and it most certainly was not the Lord. You've probably experienced something very similar when you committed to pray. It might not be washing the car, but something came into your mind, or interrupted your schedule, that tried to keep you from praying. Realizing where it comes from helps you deal with it and move on to prayer.

.: POWERFUL WEAPON :.

The opposition of Satan to prayer comes because prayer is a powerful spiritual weapon given to Christians that unleashes the power of Jesus Christ and can bring defeat to our enemy. In Ephesians 6:12, we are reminded that, "our struggle is not against flesh and blood, but against the rulers, against the authorities, against the powers of this dark world, and against the spiritual forces of evil in the heavenly realms." Defeating a spiritual enemy requires a spiritual weapon. Paul again tells us, "we do not wage war as the world does. The weapons we fight with are not the weapons of this world" (2 Corinthians 10:3-4.)

Dr Sidlow Baxter creatively pictures this struggle: "I can just imagine Satan gathering all the demons in hell and discussing what they can do to destroy Christians. And Satan says, 'Keep them from praying. Because no matter what else they do, if they don't pray, we can beat them every time. But if they learn how to pray, they'll beat us every time. Keep them from praying.'"

The enemy's attempt to stop prayer is even intensified at the congregational level. The only thing on earth more dangerous to Satan than a praying Christian is a whole church full of praying Christians! As a church begins to move into prayer together, it can expect increased opposition. "The one concern of the devil is to keep Christians from praying," said Samuel Chadwick. "He fears nothing from prayerless studies, prayerless work and prayerless religion. He laughs at our toil, mocks our wisdom, but he trembles when we pray."

Let's look at some ways that the Devil tries to prevent powerful prayer in the Church.

.: APATHY :.

First of all, he uses one of his favorite weapons: apathy. If people don't care about prayer, they will never give themselves to it. Apathy is created by a failure to understand the purpose and power of prayer. If you believe that prayer doesn't really change anything, then it won't matter much to you if you pray or don't pray. As a congregation, apathy will make prayer an option for those who desire it, and most will choose to opt out.

.: LACK OF PRAYING LEADERS :.

The lack of praying leadership is another way that prayer is thwarted on a congregational level. The church as a whole will never rise above the level of its leaders. If leaders do not see the importance and necessity of becoming a praying people, then it will not happen. In many congregations, prayer ministry is handed off to a few prayer warriors and leadership feels like they've handled the issue. What a far cry from the leaders of the Jerusalem church in the first century who handed off other issues so they could give themselves to prayer.

AS A CONGREGATION, APATHY WILL MAKE PRAYER AN OPTION FOR THOSE WHO DESIRE IT, AND MOST WILL CHOOSE TO OPT OUT.

.: FEAR :.

Fear is another great weapon of the enemy in so many areas of life, but especially in prayer. Many Christians are afraid to pray out loud. That usually keeps them from attending any sort of prayer gathering. Of course, out loud, verbal prayer is not a requirement, but its lack and the fear that goes with it is a huge detriment to becoming a praying church. To combat that, we need first of all to make our prayer gatherings safe places for those who are learning to pray. Never call on someone to pray publicly, whom you have not first checked with or whom you know has done it before.

We can also train people to pray out loud. It's not a matter of just telling them they ought to. That won't work! But we can patiently teach people to pray out loud, first of all, in their own private prayer times. Just hearing their own voices, quietly praying in private, will be a great victory and a first step in overcoming fear. One powerful way to do this is to simply read out loud the great prayers of Scripture. There is something in audibly reading/praying the Word that brings faith and overcomes fear.

.: PRIDE :.

Pride prevents prayer. If we are not in a place of humility before God, prayer will have no attraction for us. Prayer in its essence is a humbling of oneself before the Creator of all things. If a church is all about building itself up and its own accomplishments, prayer will always be a distant reality. There is no real place or need for prayer if we believe we have it all together.

.: SELF-CENTEREDNESS :.

Closely allied to pride is self-centeredness. Interestingly, self-centeredness may actually produce prayer, but it becomes all about us and not the purposes or plans of God. There are many prayer services in churches that accomplish very little because Jesus is just a spectator. He is addressed in prayer and then forgotten as the litany of our needs and wants are presented. True prayer focuses on the purposes of Jesus Christ and not simply our own desires.

.: UNFORGIVING SPIRIT :.

An unforgiving spirit is not just a hindrance for an individual in prayer, but can prevent powerful prayer in a congregation. Unforgiveness in a congregation over hurts, real or imagined, often stops people from praying because they know that things are not right. And for those who press on in prayer, but still hold on to unforgiveness, there is no promise of the Lord to hear and respond to their prayers. Forgiveness, that great gift of God, releases the healing power of the Lord and tears down the barriers that keep our prayers from being heard.

.: TRADITION:.

Although there are certainly other ways the enemy stops the Church from prayer, the last one I would share is the barrier that tradition can play. If prayer, for many years, has been a way of opening and closing meetings, or perhaps been limited to prayers within church services, then new ways of praying can become threatening. Having a new intense way of praying can seem like something that "our" church doesn't do. Leaders can show the way with grace, but firmness, that God is calling all of His people to the ministry of prayer.

In a very real sense, the ultimate tradition in the Church is that of sitting and listening. Attendance goals for a church aren't focused on anything but being there. Many church members spend their years in church, simply sitting and listening. Prayer is a real threat to that tradition. It requires doing something. And in all honesty, we recognize that when we begin to seriously pray, our years of simply sitting are at an end. Prayer will move us to act.

Once again, let us learn from saints from ages past, who dealt with satanic opposition to prayer and whose words encourage us to overcome.

"If I fail to spend two hours in prayer each morning, the devil gets the victory through the day. I have so much business I cannot get on without spending three hours daily in prayer."
—Martin Luther *(christian-prayer-quotes.christian-attorney.net)*

"Satan trembles when he sees the weakest Christian on his knees." —William Cowper

"Depend upon it, if you are bent on prayer, the devil will not leave you alone. He will molest you, tantalize you, block you, and will surely find some hindrances, big or little or both. And we sometimes fail because we are ignorant of his devices. . . . I do not think he minds our praying about things if we leave it at that. What he minds, and opposes steadily, is the prayer that prays on until it is prayed through, assured of the answer."
—Mary Warburton Booth
(awakeandgo.com)

.: POINTS TO PONDER :.

• How have you personally experienced Satan's attempt to keep you from prayer?

• Explain ways you have seen Satan try to stop congregational prayer in your church.

• Estimate what percentage of your church members are comfortable praying out loud in public.

• What are some ways your church can overcome Satan's attempt to stop prayer?

CHAPTER 8

..∥ PRAYER AND THE COMING KINGDOM ∥..

Up in a little town in Maine, things were pretty dead some years ago. The churches were not accomplishing anything. There were a few Godly men in the churches, and they said: "Here we are, only uneducated laymen; but something must be done in this town. Let us form a praying band. We will all center our prayers on one man. Who shall it be?"

They picked out one of the hardest men in town, a hopeless drunkard, and centered all their prayers upon him. In a week, he was converted. They centered their prayers upon the next hardest man in town, and soon he was converted. Then they took up another and another, until within a year, two or three hundred were brought to God, and the fire spread out into all the surrounding country. Definite prayer for those in the prison house of sin is the need of the hour.

—R. A. Torrey, from prayforrevival.wordpress.com, March 3, 2012

SEVERAL YEARS AGO I wrote a book called *Prayer and the End of Days*, in which I shared my belief that we are living close to the return of Christ. I'm not a date setter. I have no "insider" information as to the Lord's return. Biblically speaking, the entire Church Age can be called the end of days. But because I believe that Jesus might well be ready to return, I would say that we have moved into the end of the end of days.

There are some very specific reasons why I believe the Lord's return may be soon, but that's another book to write sometime. I want to share how God is calling His Church to prayer as a way of preparing for the soon return of His Son. In a very real sense, it is a John the Baptist calling . . . prepare the way for the Lord!

In most cases, God does nothing on earth relating to humans apart from prayer. When God is preparing to do something, he stirs up His people to pray. That was the case when He sent His Son into the world 2,000 years ago. He had two elderly intercessors, Anna and

PRAYER CAN NO LONGER BE SEEN AS A SIDE ISSUE, JUST FOR THE SUPER SPIRITUAL. Simeon, who were passionately praying for the coming Messiah. We have every reason to believe that He is doing the same today.

If that is the case, then there is nothing more important for the Church today than to learn to step into her role as a praying Church. Prayer can no longer be seen as a side issue, just for the super spiritual. It is at the heart of what God is desiring to do in the world today. Spirit-led prayer will center around three concepts: revival praying, evangelistic praying. and watchmen praying.

.: WAKE UP :.

God is calling His people to wake up! "Wake up, sleeper, rise from the dead, and Christ will shine on you" (Ephesians 5:14). Revival is a time when a sleeping Church wakes up and begins to experience the Presence of Christ in a fresh, new way. There is no doubt of the desperate need for revival or spiritual awakening in the Church today. Any student of revival will tell you that God always sets His people to prayer in anticipation of an awakening.

For decades, there have been those in the United States, and many other nations, who have had the foresight both to see the need for revival and to begin laying the foundation of prayer for a fresh move of God. That movement of prayer is intensifying as more and more believers are beginning to see the desperate needs of our nation and world and are understanding that only God can meet those needs. Ministries are springing up to build an increasing cry for revival in our day. Many are crying out as C. H. Spurgeon did,

"Oh! Men and brethren, what would this heart feel if I could but believe that there were some among you who would go home and pray for a revival—men whose faith is large enough, and their love fiery enough, to lead them from this moment to exercise unceasing intercessions that God would appear among us and do wondrous things here, as in the times of former generations" *(awakeandgo.com).*

Revival praying is more than just asking for revival as a part of a long list of things you want from God. It involves positioning yourself before the Lord in humility and repentance. This is a prayer that recognizes your own role in the sad condition of the Church and society and cries out for forgiveness. It is a prayer of desperation that believes the Lord's intervention is our only hope. Revival praying prepares a landing spot for the Holy Spirit to come in transformative power.

One of the great struggles in revival praying is the amount of faith required to continue steadfast in prayer. This is not a three-step plan to change the world in three weeks or less. It is a determination to pray until you see God move or you die in the effort. It is John Knox crying out, "Give me Scotland or I die!" It is a faith effort that prays regardless of what you see happening around you. It is a commitment to pray until you see fulfilled what was spoken by the prophet Habakkuk, "For the earth will be filled with the knowledge of the glory of the LORD as the waters cover the sea" (Habakkuk 2:14). John Piper said, "History testifies to the power of prayer as the prelude to spiritual awakening and missions advance."

.: EVANGELISTIC PRAYER :.

The second area of prayer that marks the end-time Church is evangelistic praying. One of the clearest indicators of the soon return of Jesus is the progress of the gospel. Jesus said in Matthew 24:14, "And this gospel of the kingdom will be preached in the whole world as a testimony to all nations, and then the end will come." We can discuss what it means for the gospel to be preached to all nations, but regardless of the position you take, Jesus ties the fulfillment of it to His return.

Martin Lloyd-Jones powerfully phrased it this way, "The main reason we should be praying about revival is that we are anxious to see God's name vindicated and His glory manifested. We should be anxious to see something happening that will arrest the nations, all the peoples, and cause them to stop and think again" *(awakeandgo.com)*.

In our day, where the Church is praying the most, it is growing the most. Prayer is fueling evangelism in amazing ways. Several years ago, my wife, Kim, and I had the opportunity to visit Indonesia for the World Prayer Assembly. It seems like a strange place for a Christian prayer gathering. Indonesia has a larger Muslim population than any other nation. But the Church there is growing rapidly, being fueled by hundreds of day and night prayer centers. Indonesians believers are coming together to pray in extraordinary ways and God is responding to their prayers. More than 20 percent of Indonesia is now Christian and the number continues to grow rapidly.

God is calling the Church to pray to the Lord of the Harvest for workers in the harvest fields of the earth. In Matthew 13:39, Jesus said, "The harvest is the end of the age." The Lord is pulling out all the stops to bring in all who are being called to Him. Our job is to pray and share, that the Lord's Body would include everyone who will respond to the message of Christ. Andrew Murray once said, "The man who mobilizes the Christian church to pray will make the greatest contribution to world evangelization in history."

∴ WATCHMEN PRAYER ∵

The third area of prayer is watchmen praying. In Old Testament culture, watchmen/guards were placed around communities for protection and to warn of danger. In Isaiah 62:6-7, God pulls together prayer and the watchmen concept for us and literally establishes this as a way of prayer. "I have posted watchmen on your walls, Jerusalem; they will never be silent day or night. You who call on the LORD, give yourselves no rest, and give him no rest till he establishes Jerusalem and makes her the praise of the earth."

The great need for a praying Church today is for those who will stand on the walls of their communities and nations and watch and pray. Watchmen pay close attention to what is happening in the world around them and, at the same time, are careful to see what is happening in the Spirit. Watchmen are asking the Lord to step into situations to bring about His will and purposes. Watchmen also sound the alarm to others, that a unified movement of praying Christians can be mobilized in times of crisis.

WATCHMEN ARE ASKING THE LORD TO STEP INTO SITUATIONS TO BRING ABOUT HIS WILL AND PURPOSES.

One of the characteristic of watchmen praying according to Isaiah, is "day and night" praying. "Never be silent day or night" demonstrates the seriousness of what it means to be a watchman. The Global Day of Prayer has established ten days and nights of continual prayer leading up to Pentecost. That is a picture of watchmen praying.

Throughout the years, Jesus Christ has stirred His people to this kind of powerful intercession and worship. The Moravians in the early 1700s were a prime example of day and night prayer. They established a 24/7 prayer meeting that lasted non-stop for more than 100 years! It resulted in a powerful missions movement.

Missionary pioneer Hudson Taylor understood this type of passionate prayer: "Since the days of Pentecost, has the whole church ever put aside every other work and waited upon Him for ten days, that the Spirit's power might be manifested? We give too much attention to method and machinery and resources, and too little to the source of power" *(awakeandgo.com)*.

In our time, day and night prayer is again becoming a mark of a praying Church. Whether the intercessory worship style of the International House of Prayer, or the 24/7 "boiler room" style that began in England under the leadership of Pete Grieg, or even the prayer towers in Indonesia, God is clearly calling His people back to extraordinary prayer. We are once again hearing Jesus say to us, "Couldn't you . . . keep watch with me [and pray] for one hour?" (Matthew 26:40).

For many reading this, the idea of day and night praying seems like a fantasy. If your church has a prayer meeting at all, it may only be attended by just a few faithful saints. My challenge to you is to not look to your circumstances, but to the vision of what God is desiring to do in us and through us. God does not despise the day of small things (Zechariah 4:10). Do not quit. Stretch your faith. Perhaps your congregation could do one week of unending prayer–168 hours. That would give your people a powerful picture of what could be.

Whether we are involved in day and night prayer, or praying for revival and world evangelization, our purpose is to agree with the teaching of Jesus that His Kingdom would come and His will would be done . . . on earth as it is in heaven. The Kingdom that Jesus declared was not of this world, is still intended to impact this world as no other kingdom ever has or will. The frontline of the advance of Christ's Kingdom is a praying Church!

.: POINTS TO PONDER :.

• How does prayer seem like a "John the Baptist" calling of preparing the way of the Lord?

• What would revival praying look like in your church?

• How has prayer impacted the evangelistic effort of your church?

• Would your congregation respond to the call to be watchmen on the walls in prayer? Why or why not? If not, how can you encourage and prepare them to respond?

CHAPTER 9

..⫽ THE PROMISES OF A PRAYING CHURCH ⫽..

A young single mom named Tammy started coming to our church at the end of the summer of 1996. She was very new to the "things of God," but wanted to help out somewhere in the church. She became a helper in Sunday school, "herding children" while the teacher concentrated on teaching the Word. It was perfect for her and for the teacher. Tammy knew the children and could help with them, while at the same time she could also learn more of the Bible.

At a training seminar for teachers and helpers one Saturday morning, Tammy showed up with a patch on her eye, obviously in terrible pain. She explained that she had been decorating her home for Halloween on the previous Thursday evening, and in a moment of revelation, realized that the decorations were primarily focused on the occult—things God condemned in the Bible. She suddenly understood that God was not pleased with that, and so she determined to take the objects down quickly. One decoration was attached to a wooden shutter by a tack with a string—and she gave it a strong yank. The tack immediately dislodged and landed in her eye.

It takes no imagination to know that Tammy screamed in pain. The damage was done. All the peripheral vision from that eye was gone, and her forward sight, marred by a scratch across the cornea, was terribly impaired. The doctor said she lost all of her side vision, and he couldn't be sure what could be recovered with her forward sight. Her vision was blurry and extremely sensitive to any kind of light.

It was a strange turn of events. This happened because Tammy believed she was obeying the Lord's command not to be involved with the occult.

An Agreeing Moment

Brent (an elder), his wife Barb, another elder named Ralph, and my wife and I listened to her story. We were all people of prayer, and more specifically, Brent, Ralph and Barb were lead-teachers of our prayer ministry. We realized that God's reputation was at stake in this matter. When someone in the group spoke up and said, "God wants to heal Tammy's eye," the five of us sensed an increase of the presence of God. His compassion began to well up inside of us.

"Tammy," Barb said, "may we pray for God to heal you?"

"Oh, please!" Tammy replied.

Our numbers had increased by now with more people walking in for the seminar. So 14 of us gathered around our friend, placed our hands upon her, and began to beseech the Lord that this attack on Tammy's new faith would not have its full effect. We prayed for God to heal and restore her eye. The manifest presence of the Lord was very tangible and palpable, while each of us in turn asked the Lord for mercy on this new believer.

"What's happening while we are praying, Tammy?" I asked.

"Fiery heat is flowing into my body and going into my eye!" she said. "The pain is subsiding!"

"Do you want us to keep praying?" someone asked.

"Oh, please!" she said.

And so we prayed for 20 minutes—until the pain completely vanished. Suddenly the intense presence of the Lord lifted, and we knew we were done. Tammy kept the patch on her eye, but all the pain and sensitivity to light disappeared. We had just experienced powerful agreement in prayer with each other.

Of course, as anyone would, Tammy went to the doctor to determine how to adapt to the damaged eye.

The doctor removed the patch. His jaw dropped.

"Doctor," she said, "what's wrong?"

"Wrong?" he said. "Why there's nothing wrong." In astonishment, he repeated, "There is absolutely nothing wrong!"

He checked her vision and found she had 20/20 vision straight ahead, with 100 percent peripheral vision on the sides.

"What did you do between Thursday and now?" he said.

"Well, on Saturday morning, 14 people asked the Lord Jesus to heal my

eye," she replied.

The doctor declared that he didn't know about Jesus, but that he knew for sure there was no longer anything wrong with her eye.

We invited Tammy to testify to the rest of the church about what the Lord had done. We were all as astonished as the doctor. The Lord healed her eye through the prayer ministry of two or three who agreed that this must be done.

If two of you agree . . . it shall be done. So says the Lord.

—David Chotka, "If Two of You . . ." Prayer Connect, *Issue 3*

A CHURCH THAT PRAYS is a place/people that attracts the Presence of God. God has always wanted His people to be with Him and to communicate with Him. In the same way that He designed the Temple as a meeting place with Himself, so has He designed the Church. God shows up in special ways where His people have chosen to spend time with Him in prayer. God rejoices over a praying church!

The Father is pleased because as a praying people, His people are walking in obedience to His Word. The Son is delighted to be enthroned as Head of the Church in practical everyday ways, instead of simply by acknowledgement. The Spirit is free to do all that the Father directs Him because their people are continually before the Throne, asking for the power of the Spirit.

Because the Lord's people are busy in prayer, all of Heaven is busy with with divine activity. Things begin to change on this planet that would not have changed had the Church not prayed. Prayer really does move the hand of God. But in addition to all the wonderful things that are released because of the praying saints, we will also see a changed Church as it becomes known for prayer.

∴ THE MARKS ∴

A praying church:
• will passionately love God

- will demonstrate love for one another in practical ways
- will have an evangelistic heart
- will care for its leaders
- will be growing in the Word
- will demonstrate the power of God
- will be concerned for its community and nation
- will nurture stronger families

Oswald Chambers said, "We have to pray with our eyes on God, not on the difficulties." A praying Church keeps its eyes on God, not on other things. It is in spending time with the Lord in prayer, especially as a congregation, that love for the Lord is deepened and enriched. It is easy to flippantly say, "I love God." It is quite another thing to demonstrate that love in close communication. Giving ourselves to the Lord in prayer is a practical manifestation of our love for Him.

You've noticed that rarely is the offer to pray for someone turned down. Even among non-believers, prayer is seen as an act of genuine love and care. When Scripture tells us to pray for one another, that becomes the practical way by which we regularly demonstrate love. If you know your church family is praying regularly for you, you know you are being loved. Augustine wrote, "Prayer is to intercede for the well-being of others before God."

John Calvin wrote, "Our prayer must not be self-centered. It must arise not only because we feel our own need as a burden we must lay upon God, but also because we are so bound up in love for our fellow men that we feel their need as acutely as our own. To make intercession for men is the most powerful and practical way in which we can express our love for them" *(chrisitan-prayer-quotes.christian-attorney.net)*.

TRAINING CHURCH MEMBERS IN EVANGELISTIC PRAYING WILL TRANSFORM YOUR CHURCH CULTURE.

When Christians are trained and motivated to pray for the lost, whether near them or far away, their hearts will be changed by the Lord. You cannot pray for those who do not know Jesus very long before everything within you becomes captured by the love of God for them. Training church members in evangelistic praying will transform your church culture. As my friend Alvin VanderGriend says, "Before we talk to men about God, we should talk to God about men."

When Christians are encouraged and trained to pray for their church leaders, criticism is replaced by intercession. Pastors and other leaders often cite constant criticism as one of the key factors in leaving a church or even the ministry. We are called by God to pray for those who are over us in the Lord. Prayer for leaders changes the atmosphere of a congregation. As someone once said, "If the church wants a better pastor, it only needs to pray for the one it has."

One of my prayer leader friends, Terry Teykl, wrote a book on praying for pastors entitled, *Preyed on or Prayed for*. All too many pastors feel preyed upon. The simplest way to change this is to understand that God calls us to intercession, not accusation. In Revelation, Satan is called the accuser of the brethren. In Romans and Hebrews, Jesus is called our Intercessor. Who do we follow . . . the accuser or the Intercessor? Praying churches are praying for their leaders.

.: PRAYING SCRIPTURE :.

The most effective way to pray is to base your prayers on the Word of God. A praying church will be one where the Word is greatly honored. The Lord's people are spending more and more time in the Word, not just reading to obtain knowledge, but praying its principles back to God. Scriptural prayers lead to a more biblically literate congregation. E.M Bounds once said, "The Word of God is the food by which prayer is nourished and made strong."

As the Word of God is prayed, the power of God will be demonstrated in fresh new ways. Most non-Christians (and sadly, Christians too) do not think of the Church in terms of power. We seem to be more about words than power. Paul said, in 1 Corinthians 2:4, that his message was not just a matter of words, but of power. Missionary pioneer J. Hudson Taylor felt the same way, "The prayer power has never been tried to its full capacity. If we want to see mighty wonders of divine power and grace wrought in the place of weakness, failure and disappointment, let us answer God's standing challenge, 'Call unto me, and I will answer

thee, and show thee great and mighty things which thou knowest not!'"
(awakeandgo.com).

Samuel Chadwick wrote,

> "There is no power like that of prevailing prayer, of Abraham pleading for Sodom, Jacob wrestling in the stillness of the night, Moses standing in the breach, Hannah intoxicated with sorrow, David heartbroken with remorse and grief, Jesus in sweat of blood. Add to this list from the records of the church your personal observation and experience, and always there is the cost of passion unto blood. Such prayer prevails. It turns ordinary mortals into men of power. It brings power. It brings fire. It brings rain. It brings life. It brings God" (awakeandgo.com).

As a congregation grows to become more mature in praying, its prayers will increasingly move from praying for church-related issues, to more outwardly related ones. Because prayer connects us to the heart of God, we will find ourselves praying for our neighborhoods, communities, and even our nation. Gaining God's perspective will overcome our tendency to pull back and just be concerned about me and mine.

"All great soul-winners have been men of much and mighty prayer," said Salvation Army leader Samuel Logan Brengle. "And all great revivals have been preceded and carried out by persevering, prevailing knee-work in the closet."

Prayer on a congregational level will always affect the families in a church. Family prayer training will show members how husbands and wives and families can pray together. As families come before the Lord together, they will be strengthened not just in their faith, but in their relationships with one another. The praying family is a stronger family in every way. If families are praying together, it is an easy step for the church family to begin to pray together.

A House of Prayer is a church that has been and is continuing to be transformed by the work of the Spirit of God as its members spend time in the Presence of the Lord. As Leonard Ravenhill said, "The true church lives and moves and has its being in prayer."

In his typical prophetic style, R. A. Torrey challenges us, "We are too busy to pray, and so we are too busy to have power. We have a great deal of activity, but we accomplish little; many services but few conversions; much machinery but few results."

We can be different! God has clearly called us to be a House of Prayer for all nations. In spite of the pressures in the modern day Church, there is time for prayer that can change the world. Andrew Murray said it this way, "Time spent in prayer will yield more than that given to work. Prayer alone gives work its worth and its success. Prayer opens the way for God Himself to do His work in us and through us. Let our chief work as God's messengers be intercession; in it we secure the presence and power of God to go with us" *(Christian-prayer-quotes.christian-attorney.net)*.

.: POINTS TO PONDER :.

• In what ways would you say your church is currently experiencing of the presence of God?

• Do you feel your church family is effective in praying for one another? Why or why not? If not, how could you improve?

• How has your congregation planned to pray for its leaders?

• Has your congregation shifted from inward-oriented prayers to outward? Are there practical ways this can increase?

APPENDIX A

·⫶ RESOURCES FOR A PRAYING CHURCH ⫶·

The following are some valuable resources that can provide help to you as you seek to become a praying church.

1. *Prayer Connect* Magazine *(www.prayerconnect.net)*. *Prayer Connect* is an award winning, full color magazine devoted to prayer that is published five times a year. Individuals, families, and churches will benefit from the practical articles from a wide variety of authors.

2. Church Prayer Leaders Network *(www.prayerleader.com)*. Interact with prayer leaders from around the world in a way that encourages, networks, and brings fresh, new ideas to help your church become a praying church. An annual membership provides *Prayer Connect* magazine and discounts on books at prayershop.org. The CPLN's website offers great ideas, including a section called, Prayer Leader Central, which has many ideas and articles to help pastors and prayer leaders in specific areas of prayer.

3. PrayerShop Bookstore *(www.prayershop.org)*. The largest prayer-only bookstore online. Browsing through PrayerShop is a delight for praying Christians who are looking for resources to help them grow in prayer.

APPENDIX B

·‖ SPECIAL DAYS OF PRAYER ‖··

NATIONAL DAY OF PRAYER *(nationaldayofprayer.org)*. Held the first Thursday of May each year, the National Day of Prayer rallies believers across the United States to pray for the nation.

CALL 2 FALL *(call2fall.com)*. A day of repentance for the Church in the U.S. on the Sunday nearest to the 4th of July.

INTERNATIONAL DAY OF PRAYER FOR THE PEACE OF JERUSALEM *(daytopray.com)*. Held the first Sunday of October each year, this day focuses on praying for Israel.

GLOBAL DAY OF PRAYER *(globaldayofprayer.com)*. This is the largest international day of prayer in the world. It takes place on Pentecost Sunday each year.

SEE YOU AT THE POLE *(syatp.com)*. Join millions of students (elementary through high school) as they gather for prayer around the flagpole of their schools on the fourth Thursday of September each year.

COLLEGIATE DAY OF PRAYER *(collegiatedayofprayer.org)*. Thousands of colleges and universities are prayed for each year on the last Thursday of February.

INTERNATIONAL DAY OF PRAYER FOR THE PERSECUTED CHURCH *(idop.org)*. Christians around the world pray for their persecuted brothers and sisters in Christ on the second Sunday in November.

CRY OUT AMERICA *(awakeningamerica.us)*. People gather on September 11 each year and focus prayer on their cities, counties, states, and the nation.

··‖ NATIONAL PRAYER ACCORD ‖··

The National Prayer Accord is patterned after a rhythm of prayer established by Jonathan Edwards and churches in the colonies prior to the first great awakening in the United States. In more recent days, many prayer and revival ministries are encouraging believers and churches to adopt this ongoing rhythm of prayer in their own circles.

In Recognition of:
- Our absolute dependence on God

- The moral and spiritual challenges facing our nation

- Our national need for repentance and divine intervention

- The covenants of prayer that God has answered throughout history

- Our great hope for a general awakening to the Lordship of Christ, the unity of His Body, and the sovereignty of His Kingdom

We strongly urge all churches and followers of Jesus in America to unite in seeking the face of God through prayer and fasting, persistently asking our Father to send revival to the Church and spiritual awakening to our nation so that Christ's Great Commission might be fulfilled worldwide in our generation.

This voluntary agreement in prayer seems "good to the Holy Spirit and to us" (Acts 15:28) in light of the promise of Jesus in Matthew 18:19 and the unity for which Jesus prayed in John 17. This prayer accord presupposes a spirit of freedom to adjust its component parts as local Christians see need.

Though many are seeking God more often than this prayer accord outlines, calling millions of others around focused times of prayer is an urgent need.

.: WE RESOLVE TO PROMOTE AS AN ONGOING :. "RHYTHM OF PRAYER". · ·

WEEKLY . . . In private or small group prayer, which lends itself to a focus on the regular preaching and teaching of God's Word, asking the Holy Spirit to light the fires of revival by anointing our preachers and teachers each week.

MONTHLY . . . In local ministry prayer gatherings, such as a mid-week prayer meeting, a Bible study class, a Sunday evening service, a home group, or one meeting of a college campus group, etc. for the exclusive purpose of prayer for revival.

QUARTERLY . . . In prayer gatherings among local ministries and groups, uniting churches in a community, college ministries in the area, businessmen's groups, or radio listeners for an evening meeting, a luncheon, or a segment of airtime focusing on prayer for the community or region.

ANNUALLY . . . In prayer meetings designed to unite Christians nationally, such as The National Day of Prayer, the first Thursday of May, and Cry Out America, on September 11, each year—occasions that call millions of people to pray together.

The National Prayer Committee and its partners offer tools, templates, and stories to help facilitate this prayer accord *(www.nationalprayeraccord. com)*, while recommending that other ministries do the same.

Downstream in America we find the symptoms and signs of church irrelevance, fragmented relationships, cultural decay, moral decline, and love growing cold, but Upstream from such symptoms, we find hope in united prevailing prayer.

> "... but I have prayed for you and when you are restored strengthen others" (Luke 22:32).

As certainly as Jesus prayed for Peter, He prays for us!

"Jesus Christ is the same yesterday and today, yes forever"
(Hebrews 13:8).

"He always lives to make intercession"(Hebrews 7:25).

"Christ Jesus is He...who also intercedes for us"(Romans 8:33).

We resolve to promote as "Prayer Goals" the outpouring of God's Spirit for . . .

∴ THE REVIVAL OF THE CHURCH AS EVIDENCED BY ∴ THE INDICATORS OF AWAKENING IN THE CHURCH

1. Increasing testimony of the manifest presence of God.

2. Increased conversions and baptisms.

3. Amplified participation in corporate as well as individual prayer, fasting, and other spiritual disciplines leading to more effective discipleship.

4. A decrease in divorces and renewed commitment to marriage between a man and a woman in covenant relationship as God intends.

5. Imparting faith to children and youth as parents are equipped by the church to become primary disciplers of their children.

6. Among churches, a passionate pursuit for the well-being of their cities through the planting of new congregations, benevolent ministries, practical service, and focused evangelism.

7. Commitment to radical generosity as evidenced by compassion ministries and global missions.

8. Improved health among ministers as evidenced by their joy, decreased resignations, healthy loving relationships within their families, and an increased response among young

people called to the ministry.

9. Christians involved in bold witness accompanied by miracles, dramatic conversions, and Holy Spirit empowered victories over evil.

10. Heightened expressions of love and unity among all believers, as demonstrated by the unity of pastors and leaders.

THE ADVANCEMENT OF THE KINGDOM .: AS EVIDENCED BY THESE INDICATORS OF :. AWAKENING IN THE CULTURE

1. Breakdowns of racial, social and status barriers as Christ's church celebrates Jesus together!

2. A restoration of morality, ethical foundations and accountability among leaders of church and government, business and politics.

3. A transformation of society through the restoration of Christ's influence in the arts, media, and communications.

4. Increased care for the hungry and homeless, the most vulnerable and needy.

5. Young adults, students, and children embracing the claims and lifestyle of Christ through the witness of peers who live and love as Jesus did.

6. Community and national leaders seeking out the church as an answer to society's problems.

7. Increased care for children as "gifts from the Lord" as the gospel addresses abortion, adoption, foster care, and child well-being.

8. Righteous relations between men and women: decrease in divorce rates, cohabitation, same-sex relations, sexual abuse, sexual trafficking, out-of-wedlock children, and STDs.

9. An awakening to the "fear of the Lord" rather than the approval of people, thus restoring integrity and credibility.

10. Neighborhood transformation and an accompanying decrease of social ills through increased expressions of "loving your neighbor" in service, compassion, and unity.

Developed by America's National Prayer Committee in partnership with OneCry and the Awakening America Alliance.

..‖ START THE DISCUSSION ‖..

Use *Forgotten Power* to begin a discussion among your staff, elders, deacons or board on what a praying church looks like. Let it stimulate your church in its desire to become more kingdom-focused.

Available through your local Christian bookstore or outlets.
Also available in e-book format.

Multiple copy discounts are available on as few as five copies at *prayershop.org.*

PRAYERCONNECT

Connecting to the Heart of Christ through Prayer

  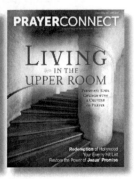

A NEW BIMONTHLY MAGAZINE DESIGNED TO:

Equip prayer leaders and pastors with tools to disciple their congregations.

Connect intercessors with the growing worldwide prayer movement.

Mobilize believers to pray God's purposes for their church, city and the nations.

Each issue of *Prayer Connect* includes:
- Practical articles to equip and inspire your prayer life.
- Helpful prayer tips and proven ideas.
- News of prayer movements around the world.
- Theme articles exploring important prayer topics.
- Connections to prayer resources available online.

Print subscription: $24.99 (includes digital version)

Digital subscription: $19.99

Church Prayer Leaders Network membership: $30 (includes print, digital, and CPLN membership benefits)

Subscribe now.
Order at www.prayerconnect.net or call 800-217-5200.

PRAYERCONNECT *is sponsored by: America's National Prayer Committee, Denominational Prayer Leaders Network and The International Prayer Council.*

CPSIA information can be obtained at www.ICGtesting.com
Printed in the USA
LVOW08s1121280715

447933LV00024B/269/P